LIFE CHANGING SALADS COOKBOOK

2000 DAYS OF FRESH, NOURISHING RECIPES TO BOOST ENERGY AND HEALTH

Published by
GRAPEVINE BOOKS

www.grapevinebooks.com
email: contact@grapevinebooks.com

Ordering Information:
Quantity sales: Special discounts are available on quantity purchases
by corporations, associations, and others.
For details, reach out to the publisher.

First published by Grapevine Books, 2026

Get Your Free E-book!

Scan the QR code below to instantly access the e-book **'The Salad Builder Blueprint'**, absolutely free

SCAN ME

https://bonus.grapevinebooks.com/saladbuilder

CONTENTS

Hey there!

Welcome to your ultimate guide to fresh, vibrant, real food —a salad book like no other. Whether you're here to reboot your habits, fuel your workouts, or simply fall back in love with vegetables, this collection has something for every craving and every lifestyle.

How to Use This Book: Recipes are grouped by wellness goals—detox, gut health, energy, weight loss, immune support, and more. Flip to any section that matches your needs, mood, or pantry and dive in.

The Power of Plant-Based Eating: Even if you're not fully vegetarian, adding more plant-forward meals can reduce inflammation, balance blood sugar, and boost long-term energy.

Pantry Staples & Prep Tips: Keep lemon, olive oil, grains, beans, and a few key greens on hand, and you can whip up nearly any salad in this book with ease.

Why Salads? Why Now? Because they're fast. They're versatile. And when done right, they're one of the most powerful tools for feeling better, every single day.

Recipe Labels

30 = ready in 30 minutes or less
h = great for hosting or serving to guests
lf = stores well and makes tasty leftovers
nc = no cooking required at all
nf = made without any nuts
sf = contains no soy ingredients

CHAPTER 1

SPRING GREENS & GUT HEALTH

1

Apple Cabbage Salad

SERVES 4

This crunchy, vibrant salad is your gut's best friend.

30 ⏱ | nc | nf |

prep time: **15 minutes**

cook time: **5 minutes**

2 cups shredded green cabbage
1 cup shredded red cabbage
1 crisp apple thinly sliced
1 small carrot, julienned
2 tbsp lemon juice
1 tbsp apple cider vinegar
1 tbsp extra virgin olive oil
1 tsp maple syrup (optional)
2 tbsp chopped fresh parsley
Salt, black pepper to taste
1 tbsp sunflower seeds (optional topping)

1. In a large bowl, combine the green cabbage, red cabbage, apple slices, and carrot.
2. In a small jar, shake together the lemon juice, apple cider vinegar, olive oil, maple syrup (if using), salt, and pepper until well mixed.
3. Pour the dressing over the salad and toss to coat evenly.
4. Let it sit for 5-10 minutes to soften and blend flavors.
5. Garnish with parsley and sunflower seeds before serving.

This salad stores well in the fridge for up to 3 days.
Add nuts or chickpeas for a heartier version or enjoy as-is.

Cucumber Dill Salad

SERVES 4

Cool, crisp, and delightfully refreshing.

30 ⏱ | nc | sf

prep time: **10 minutes**

cook time: **5 minutes**

2 large cucumbers, thinly sliced
2 tbsp fresh dill, finely chopped
¼ cup red onion, thinly sliced
1 tbsp apple cider vinegar
1 tbsp lemon juice
1 tbsp olive oil
Salt and pepper to taste
(Optional) 2 tbsp plain dairy-free yogurt for creaminess

1. In a large bowl, toss together the cucumbers, red onion, and chopped dill.

2. In a small bowl or jar, whisk together the vinegar, lemon juice, olive oil, salt, and pepper.

3. Pour the dressing over the cucumber mixture and toss until coated.

4. Chill in the fridge for at least 10 minutes before serving.

Want to make it creamy? Stir in a spoonful of dairy-free yogurt right before serving.

Chickpea Protein Bowl

SERVES 2-3

Satisfying, plant-based power meal.

30 ⏱ | h | sf

prep time: **20 minutes** cook time: **None**

1½ cups cooked or canned chickpeas, rinsed and drained
1 cup shredded red cabbage
1 cup cherry tomatoes, halved
1 cup cucumber, diced
½ avocado, sliced
¼ cup chopped fresh parsley
1 tbsp olive oil
Juice of ½ lemon
Salt and pepper to taste

For the tahini dressing:
2 tbsp tahini
1 tbsp lemon juice
1 tsp maple syrup
1 tbsp water (more as needed for consistency)
Pinch of garlic powder and salt

1. In a large bowl or serving container, arrange the chickpeas, cabbage, tomatoes, cucumber, avocado, and parsley in sections or layers.

2. In a small bowl, whisk together all tahini dressing ingredients until smooth. Add more water if needed to thin.

3. Drizzle the dressing over the bowl and season with olive oil, lemon juice, salt, and pepper.

4. Serve immediately, or store components separately for a quick, easy prep lunch.

Feel free to bulk this up with quinoa or swap avocado for olives.

Cucumber Yogurt Salad

SERVES 4

Perfect for a quick reset or clean-eating meal.

30 ⏱ | nc | nf

prep time: **10 minutes**　cook time: **None**

2 cups cucumber, thinly sliced
1 cup plain Greek yogurt (or dairy-free alternative)
1 tbsp chopped fresh dill
1 tsp lemon juice
½ garlic clove, finely grated or minced
Salt and black pepper to taste
Optional: drizzle of olive oil or pinch of cumin for flavor variation

1. In a medium bowl, combine the yogurt, lemon juice, garlic, dill, salt, and pepper. Stir to mix well.
2. Fold in the sliced cucumbers and toss gently until evenly coated.
3. Let the salad chill in the fridge for 10-15 minutes before serving to allow flavors to develop.
4. Serve cold as a light side, dip, or refreshing contrast to spicy meals.

For extra crunch and fiber, add chopped celery or grated carrots. Swap in coconut yogurt to keep it fully dairy-free and plant-based.

Beet Apple Gut Reset Salad

SERVES 5

Total gut health hero.

30 ⏱ | nc | lf

prep time: **15 minutes**

cook time: **None** (use pre-cooked or steamed beets)

3 medium cooked beets, peeled and diced
2 crisp apples, diced (like Fuji or Pink Lady)
1½ tbsp lemon juice
2 tsp apple cider vinegar
1½ tbsp extra virgin olive oil
2 tbsp chopped parsley or mint
Salt and pepper to taste
Optional: 2 tbsp pumpkin seeds or sunflower seeds

1. In a bowl, combine the diced beets and apples.
2. In a small cup, whisk together the lemon juice, vinegar, olive oil, salt, and pepper.
3. Pour the dressing over the salad and mix gently.
4. Garnish with parsley (or mint) and sprinkle seeds on top, if using.
5. Let sit for 5-10 minutes before serving to allow flavors to meld.

Stores well for up to 2 days and is perfect as a leftover lunch. Add lentils or chickpeas to turn it into a hearty detox bowl.

Citrus Avocado Detox Salad

SERVES 4

A light, zesty immunity lift.

30 ⏱ | nc | sf

prep time: **10 minutes**

cook time: **None**

1 large grapefruit, segmented
1 orange, segmented
1 ripe avocado, sliced
2 cups baby spinach or arugula
¼ red onion, thinly sliced
1 tbsp chopped fresh mint (optional)
1 tbsp olive oil
1 tsp lemon juice
Salt and pepper to taste

1. In a bowl, combine the citrus segments, avocado, onion, and greens.
2. Drizzle with olive oil and lemon juice.
3. Toss gently to coat without breaking the avocado.
4. Season with salt, pepper, and fresh mint (if using).
5. Serve immediately while fresh and chilled.

Best served fresh. Add hemp seeds or sunflower seeds for extra crunch and immune support.

Edamame Red Cabbage Slaw

SERVES 4

Crunchy, colorful, and protein-packed.

30 ⏱ | lf | sf

prep time: **15 minutes**

cook time: **None** (edamame should be thawed if frozen)

2 cups shredded red cabbage
1 cup cooked edamame (shelled)
1 carrot, grated
¼ cup green onions, sliced
1 tbsp chopped cilantro
1 tbsp lime juice
1 tbsp rice vinegar
1 tsp grated fresh ginger
1 tbsp olive oil
Salt and pepper to taste
Optional: sesame seeds for garnish

1. In a large bowl, combine the red cabbage, edamame, carrot, green onions, and cilantro.
2. In a separate bowl, whisk together lime juice, rice vinegar, ginger, olive oil, salt, and pepper.
3. Pour the dressing over the slaw and toss to combine.
4. Chill for 10 minutes before serving.
5. Garnish with sesame seeds if desired.

This salad holds up great for lunch the next day.
An excellent base for grilled tofu or avocado.

Waldorf Chicken Salad

SERVES 4

Maintains energy and weight levels without compromising flavor.

30 ⏱ | lf | nf

prep time: **15 minutes**

cook time: **None** (if chicken is pre-cooked)

2 cups cooked chicken breast, chopped or shredded
1 crisp apple, diced
½ cup seedless grapes, halved
½ cup celery, thinly sliced
¼ cup chopped walnuts (optional)
¼ cup plain Greek yogurt (or dairy-free yogurt alternative)
1 tsp lemon juice
Salt and black pepper to taste
Butter lettuce leaves (for serving)

1. In a large bowl, combine the chicken, apple, grapes, celery, and walnuts (if using).

2. In a small bowl, whisk together the yogurt, lemon juice, salt, and pepper.

3. Pour the dressing over the salad mixture and toss until well coated.

4. Serve chilled, on a bed of butter lettuce, or scoop into wraps or pita pockets for an on-the-go lunch.

This salad stores well for up to 3 days in the fridge. Just keep the lettuce separate to avoid sogginess. For a dairy-free version, use almond or coconut yogurt.

Cold Pea and Mint Salad

SERVES 4

Simple, fast, and refreshingly light.

30 | nc | nf

prep time: **10 minutes**

cook time: **None** (if using thawed frozen peas))

2 cups green peas (fresh or thawed frozen)
2 tbsp finely chopped fresh mint
1 tbsp olive oil
1 tsp lemon juice
Salt and pepper to taste
Optional: 2 tbsp crumbled feta or vegan cheese

1. In a medium bowl, combine peas and chopped mint.
2. Add olive oil, lemon juice, salt, and pepper.
3. Toss gently to combine.
4. Chill for 10-15 minutes before serving.

Great low-calorie side. To make it heartier, toss in cooked quinoa, or top with sliced avocado.

Fennel Apple Detox Salad

SERVES 4

Simple, fast, and refreshingly light.

30 | nc | sf

prep time: **10 minutes**

cook time: **None** (if using thawed frozen peas)

1 bulb fennel, halved and thinly sliced
1 crisp green apple, julienned
1 tbsp lemon juice
1 tsp apple cider vinegar
1 tbsp olive oil
Salt and black pepper to taste
Optional: fennel fronds for garnish

1. In a bowl, toss the fennel and apple slices together.
2. In a small cup, whisk the lemon juice, vinegar, olive oil, salt, and pepper.
3. Pour the dressing over the salad and mix well.
4. Garnish with chopped fennel fronds if available.
5. Chill briefly before serving for maximum flavor.

This salad is especially helpful after salty or heavy meals.

CHAPTER 2

SPRING INTO ENERGY & LIGHT MEALS

Sweet Potato Nourish Bowl

SERVES 5

Delivers plant-based energy, rich fiber, and slow-burning carbs.

h | lf | df

prep time: **20 minutes**

cook time: **30 minutes**

2 medium sweet potatoes, cubed
1 tbsp olive oil
1 tsp paprika
Salt and pepper to taste
3 cups cooked brown rice or quinoa
2 cups baby spinach or kale
1 avocado, sliced
½ cup shredded carrots
¼ cup pumpkin seeds or sunflower seeds

For the tahini dressing:
3 tbsp tahini
2 tbsp lemon juice
1 tsp maple syrup
2-3 tbsp warm water
Pinch of garlic powder and sea salt

1. Preheat oven to 400°F (200°C). Toss cubed sweet potatoes with olive oil, paprika, salt, and pepper. Roast for 25-30 minutes until golden and tender.

2. Meanwhile, prep dressing: whisk together tahini, lemon juice, maple syrup, water, and seasoning until smooth.

3. In a bowl, layer the grain, greens, roasted sweet potato, carrots, and avocado.

4. Drizzle with dressing and sprinkle seeds on top.

5. Serve warm or chilled.

Keeps well for 2-3 days. Add chickpeas or tofu for extra protein or swap spinach for kale to match your greens. preference.

High Protein Tomato Basil Salad

SERVES 5

A vibrant twist on Caprese. Simple, clean, and protein-rich.

30 | h | vgn

prep time: **15 minutes**

cook time: **None**

4-5 ripe tomatoes, chopped or sliced
1½ cups cooked white beans (cannellini or navy beans)
¼ cup fresh basil leaves, torn or sliced
1 tbsp olive oil
1 tbsp lemon juice
Salt and black pepper to taste
Optional: pinch of chili flakes or drizzle of balsamic glaze

1. In a bowl, combine tomatoes, white beans, and basil.
2. Drizzle with olive oil and lemon juice.
3. Season with salt, pepper, and chili flakes if using.
4. Toss gently and let rest for 5-10 minutes before serving.

Great summer light meal or protein-rich side.
For more texture, add cucumber or toasted seeds.

Roasted Chickpea & Sweet Potato Salad

SERVES 4

Fantastic way to support metabolism, gut health, and energy.

lf | df | sf

prep time: **20 minutes**

cook time: **30 minutes**

1 (15 oz) can chickpeas, drained, rinsed, and patted dry
2 medium sweet potatoes, peeled and cubed
1½ tbsp olive oil
1 tsp smoked paprika
½ tsp cumin
Salt and pepper to taste
4 cups mixed greens (like spinach, kale, arugula)
¼ red onion, thinly sliced

For the tahini dressing:
2 tbsp tahini
1½ tbsp lemon juice
1 tsp maple syrup
2 tbsp water (to thin)
Pinch of salt

1. Preheat oven to 400°F (200°C). Toss chickpeas and sweet potato cubes with olive oil, paprika, cumin, salt, and pepper.

2. Spread on a baking sheet and roast for 25-30 minutes, shaking halfway through, until golden and crisp.

3. Meanwhile, whisk all dressing ingredients together in a small bowl.

4. In a large bowl, combine greens and onion. Top with roasted chickpeas and sweet potatoes.

5. Drizzle with dressing and serve warm or at room temperature.

Cranberry Walnut Salad

SERVES 5

Light, flavorful, and endlessly customizable.

nc | h | vgt

prep time: **15 minutes**

cook time: **None**

5 cups mixed greens (baby spinach, arugula, or spring mix)
½ cup dried cranberries (unsweetened preferred)
½ cup walnuts, toasted and chopped
¼ cup red onion, thinly sliced
2 tbsp balsamic vinegar
1 tbsp olive oil
Salt and pepper to taste
Optional: 2 tbsp crumbled feta or goat cheese

1. In a large salad bowl, combine greens, cranberries, walnuts, and onion.
2. Drizzle with olive oil and balsamic vinegar.
3. Season with salt and pepper. Toss gently.
4. Add cheese if using and serve immediately.

For extra protein, add chickpeas or grilled chicken.
Great side for holiday meals or hearty grain bowls.

Asian Noodle Salad

SERVES 4

Perfect as a light main or chilled lunch bowl.
Supports clean eating, energy, and easy prep.

lf | sf | vgn

prep time: **20 minutes**

cook time: **10 minutes**

8 oz rice noodles, cooked and cooled
1 cup shredded red cabbage
1 cup shredded carrots
½ red bell pepper, thinly sliced
½ cucumber, julienned
2 green onions, sliced
2 tbsp sesame seeds (optional)
2 tbsp chopped cilantro

For the dressing:

2 tbsp sesame oil
1 tbsp rice vinegar
1 tbsp soy sauce or tamari
1 tsp maple syrup
1 tsp grated fresh ginger
Juice of ½ lime

1. Cook noodles according to package instructions. Rinse with cold water and drain.
2. In a large bowl, toss noodles with cabbage, carrots, bell pepper, cucumber, green onions, and cilantro.
3. In a small bowl, whisk together all dressing ingredients until smooth.
4. Pour dressing over noodle mixture and toss to combine.
5. Garnish with sesame seeds and chill before serving.

Keeps well for up to 2 days. For extra protein, add edamame, baked tofu, or shredded chicken.

Grapefruit & Avocado Salad

SERVES 5

Great for light spreads that feel indulgent but are 100% real food.

nc | df | h

prep time: **15 minutes**

cook time: **None**

- 2 large grapefruits, segmented
- 2 ripe avocados, sliced
- 5 cups baby spinach or arugula
- ¼ red onion, very thinly sliced
- 1 tbsp olive oil
- 1 tsp lemon juice or white wine vinegar
- Salt and black pepper to taste
- Optional: 1 tbsp chopped fresh mint or basil

1. In a large bowl or platter, layer spinach, grapefruit segments, avocado slices, and red onion.
2. Drizzle with olive oil and lemon juice or vinegar.
3. Sprinkle with salt, pepper, and herbs (if using).
4. Serve immediately for freshest texture and flavor.

For extra crunch, sprinkle sunflower or pumpkin seeds just before serving.

Carrot Ginger Salad

SERVES 5

Go-to for resetting your system or adding zip to any plate.

30 ⏱ | nc | nf

prep time: **15 minutes**

cook time: **None**

4 large carrots, peeled and shredded or julienned
1 tbsp fresh ginger, finely grated
1 tbsp lemon or lime juice
1 tbsp rice vinegar
1 tbsp olive oil or sesame oil
1 tsp maple syrup (optional)
Salt and pepper to taste
Optional: pinch of chili flakes or sesame seeds

1. In a mixing bowl, combine carrots and grated ginger.
2. In a small jar, shake or whisk together the lemon/lime juice, vinegar, oil, maple syrup, salt, and pepper.
3. Pour dressing over carrots and toss to combine.
4. Let sit 5-10 minutes before serving for maximum flavor.
5. Top with sesame seeds or chili flakes if desired.

Stores well for up to 3 days.
Makes a great topping for grain bowls or wraps.

Edamame Broccoli Salad

SERVES 3

With every bite, you get bold texture & gut-friendly greens.

lf | sf | vgn

prep time:
15 minutes

cook time:
5 minutes
(for blanching broccoli, optional)

1½ cups small broccoli florets (raw or briefly blanched)
1 cup cooked edamame (shelled)
⅓ red bell pepper, diced
2 tbsp shredded carrots
1 green onion, sliced
1 tsp sesame seeds

For the dressing:
1 tbsp toasted sesame oil
1 tbsp rice vinegar
1 tsp soy sauce or tamari
1 tsp lemon juice
½ tsp maple syrup
Pinch of grated garlic or ginger

1. In a large bowl, combine broccoli, edamame, bell pepper, carrots, and green onion.
2. In a small bowl, whisk together all dressing ingredients until smooth.
3. Pour the dressing over the salad and toss to coat evenly.
4. Sprinkle with sesame seeds and serve chilled or at room temperature.

For extra crunch, add chopped almonds or sunflower seeds. To turn it into a full meal, serve over quinoa or with baked tofu.

Red Cabbage Slaw with Carrot

SERVES 3

Big on fiber, light on prep, and perfect for your gut health.

nc | nf | vgn

prep time: **10 minutes**

cook time: **None**

1½ cups shredded red cabbage
¾ cup shredded carrots
1 tbsp lime juice
1 tbsp apple cider vinegar
1 tbsp olive oil
½ tsp maple syrup (optional)
Salt and pepper to taste
Optional: chopped parsley or cilantro for garnish

1. In a medium bowl, combine red cabbage and carrots.
2. In a small jar or bowl, whisk together lime juice, vinegar, olive oil, maple syrup, salt, and pepper.
3. Pour dressing over vegetables and toss well.
4. Let it sit for 5-10 minutes to soften slightly and meld flavors.
5. Garnish with herbs if desired.

This slaw keeps its crunch for a few days in the fridge. Serve over tacos, wrap it into sandwiches, or pair with grilled plant-based protein.

Zucchini Ribbon Salad

SERVES 3

Perfect summer salad and naturally low calorie.

nc | df | vgt

prep time: **10 minutes**

cook time: **None**

2 medium zucchini, shaved into ribbons using a peeler
1 tbsp lemon juice
1 tbsp olive oil
Salt and pepper to taste
Optional: 1 tbsp chopped fresh mint or basil
Optional: shaved Parmesan or vegan cheese alternative

1. Using a vegetable peeler, shave zucchini into long ribbons.

2. In a bowl, toss ribbons gently with lemon juice, olive oil, salt, and pepper.

3. Add herbs and cheese if using.

4. Let sit 5 minutes before serving to soften slightly and absorb flavor.

For extra texture, add toasted almonds or pumpkin seeds. Best enjoyed fresh but can be refrigerated for up to 1 day.

CHAPTER 3

SUMMER HYDRATION & GLOW BOWLS

Tomato Basil & Mozzarella Salad

SERVES 2

Great for sharing or savoring solo with crusty bread.

nc | h | vgt

prep time: **10 minutes**

cook time: **None**

2 ripe tomatoes, sliced
1 ball fresh mozzarella (or vegan mozzarella), sliced
¼ cup fresh basil leaves
1 tbsp olive oil
1 tsp balsamic vinegar or glaze
Salt and black pepper to taste

1. Arrange alternating slices of tomato and mozzarella on a serving plate.
2. Tuck basil leaves between the slices or scatter on top.
3. Drizzle with olive oil and balsamic.
4. Sprinkle with salt and freshly ground pepper. Serve immediately.

This salad is best made with high-quality, seasonal tomatoes. Add avocado slices or hemp seeds for extra nourishment and texture.

Sunshine Fruit Salad

SERVES 4

Vibrant medley of tropical and seasonal fruits.

gf | h | df | sf

prep time: **10 minutes**

cook time: **None**

1 cup diced pineapple
1 cup sliced strawberries
1 cup peeled and sliced oranges or mandarins
½ cup halved red grapes
½ cup diced kiwi
1 tbsp lime juice
1 tsp honey or maple syrup
Optional: chopped mint leaves

1. Combine all fruits in a large mixing bowl.

2. In a small dish, whisk together lime juice and honey or maple syrup.

3. Drizzle dressing over the fruit and toss gently.

4. Add chopped mint if desired and chill before serving.

Best served cold.
Great for picnics, parties, or post-workout refreshment.

Orange Fennel Hydration Salad

SERVES 5

Summer glow in every bite.

nc | df | vgn

prep time: **15 minutes**

cook time: **None**

2 large oranges, peeled and thinly sliced into rounds or half-moons
1 medium fennel bulb, halved and thinly sliced (reserve fronds for garnish)
¼ red onion, thinly sliced
1 tbsp olive oil
1 tbsp lemon juice
Salt and black pepper to taste
Optional: a few fennel fronds or fresh mint leaves for topping

1. In a large bowl, combine orange slices, fennel, and red onion.
2. Drizzle with olive oil and lemon juice.
3. Season with salt and pepper and toss gently.
4. Garnish with fennel fronds or mint and serve chilled or at room temperature.

This salad is high in vitamin C and naturally cooling. For a heartier version, add avocado slices or a handful of arugula.

Quinoa Tabbouleh

SERVES 4

Cooling, detox-friendly salad that's perfect for light meals.

df | vgn

prep time: **20 minutes**

cook time: **15 minutes** (to cook quinoa)

1 cup cooked quinoa, cooled
½ cup finely chopped parsley
¼ cup chopped fresh mint
1 cup diced cucumber
½ cup diced tomato
2 green onions, finely sliced
2 tbsp lemon juice
1 tbsp olive oil
Salt and pepper to taste

1. In a large bowl, combine quinoa, parsley, mint, cucumber, tomato, and green onions.
2. In a small bowl, whisk together lemon juice, olive oil, salt, and pepper.
3. Pour dressing over salad and toss to mix thoroughly.
4. Chill for 15-20 minutes before serving for maximum flavor.

Travels well. Great addition to meal prep bowls. Add chickpeas or avocado for extra heartiness.

Tomato, Cucumber & Onion Salad

SERVES 6

Staple of clean eating, perfect for summer gatherings.

nc | h | vgt

prep time: **10 minutes**

cook time: **None**

3 cups chopped cucumbers
3 cups chopped tomatoes
½ red onion, thinly sliced
2 tbsp olive oil
1½ tbsp red wine vinegar or lemon juice
Salt and black pepper to taste
Optional: 2 tbsp chopped parsley or basil

1. In a large bowl, combine cucumbers, tomatoes, and onion.
2. Drizzle with olive oil and vinegar or lemon juice.
3. Toss well to coat.
4. Season with salt and pepper. Garnish with herbs if using.
5. Chill for 10 minutes or serve immediately.

Great low-calorie, hydrating option.
Pairs well with grilled mains or whole grain bowls.

Mushroom Spinach Salad

SERVES 2

Perfect as a light main or nourishing side dish.

30 ⏱ | lf | vgt

prep time: **10 minutes**

cook time: **10 minutes**

2 cups baby spinach
1 cup sliced mushrooms (cremini or button)
1 tsp olive oil
1 tsp balsamic vinegar
½ tsp Dijon mustard
Salt and pepper to taste
Optional: shaved Parmesan or sunflower seeds

1. Heat olive oil in a skillet over medium heat. Sauté mushrooms for 5-7 minutes until tender and golden.
2. In a small bowl, whisk together balsamic vinegar, mustard, salt, and pepper.
3. In a serving bowl, place the spinach and top with warm mushrooms.
4. Drizzle with dressing and toss gently. Add toppings if desired.

Can be enjoyed warm or cold. Double the mushrooms and serve over grains for a more filling bowl.

Caesar Salad with Greek Yogurt Dressing

SERVES 4

A lighter take on the classic Caesar.

h | df | vgt

prep time: **15 minutes**

cook time: **None**

1 large head romaine lettuce, chopped
½ cup Greek yogurt
1 tbsp olive oil
1 tbsp lemon juice
1 tsp Dijon mustard
1 tsp Worcestershire sauce (or tamari for vegetarian)
1 clove garlic, finely minced
Salt and pepper to taste
1 cup whole grain croutons
Optional: grated Parmesan or vegan cheese

1. In a bowl, whisk together yogurt, olive oil, lemon juice, mustard, Worcestershire, garlic, salt, and pepper.

2. In a large salad bowl, add romaine and toss with dressing until evenly coated.

3. Top with croutons and cheese if using. Serve immediately.

For a full meal, add grilled tofu, chickpeas, or hard-boiled eggs. Keeps well in the fridge if dressing is stored separately.

Fattoush Salad

SERVES 6

This classic Middle Eastern salad is perfect for big batches.

30 | nc | vgn

prep time:
20 minutes

cook time:
None
(toasted pita optional)

2 cups chopped romaine or mixed greens
1 cup chopped cucumber
1 cup chopped tomatoes
½ red onion thinly sliced
1 cup toasted pita chips or strips
2 tbsp chopped parsley
1 tbsp olive oil
1½ tbsp lemon juice
1 tsp ground sumac (optional but authentic)
Salt and pepper to taste

1. In a large bowl, combine all vegetables, parsley, and toasted pita.
2. In a small bowl, whisk together olive oil, lemon juice, sumac, salt, and pepper.
3. Drizzle dressing over salad and toss gently.
4. Serve immediately to keep pita crunchy.

To make it heartier, add chickpeas or chopped avocado.

Avocado Spinach Mint Salad

SERVES 2

A go-to when you want something soothing, simple, and deeply nourishing.

nc | df | vgn

prep time: **10 minutes**

cook time: **None**

2 cups baby spinach
1 ripe avocado, sliced
1 tbsp chopped fresh mint
1 tbsp lemon juice
1 tsp olive oil
Salt and pepper to taste
Optional: pinch of hemp seeds or sunflower seeds

1. In a bowl, gently toss the spinach, avocado, and mint.
2. Drizzle with lemon juice and olive oil.
3. Season with salt and pepper.
4. Serve immediately for best texture.

Great on its own or paired with a grain bowl. This salad is light but full of mood-boosting and skin-glowing nutrients.

Blueberry Peach Salad

SERVES 5

Summery salad with soft sweetness.

lf | nc | vgt

prep time: **10 minutes**

cook time: **None**

4 cups arugula or spinach
2 ripe peaches, thinly sliced
¾ cup fresh blueberries
2 tbsp chopped walnuts or pecans
1 tbsp lemon juice
1 tsp honey (or maple syrup for vegan)
1 tbsp olive oil
Salt and pepper to taste

1. In a bowl, combine greens, peaches, blueberries, and nuts.
2. In a small jar, shake lemon juice, honey, olive oil, salt, and pepper.
3. Drizzle over salad and toss gently.
4. Serve immediately or chill briefly.

Add goat cheese or crumbled feta for richness, or quinoa for extra staying power.

Chapter 4

SUMMER SUPERFOODS & WEIGHT LOSS

Avocado & Corn Crunch

SERVES 4

Creamy, crunchy, and spicy.

lf | df | vgn

prep time: **15 minutes**

cook time: **None**

1 ripe avocado, diced
1 cup roasted or grilled corn (fresh or frozen)
1 cup shredded cabbage or slaw mix
¾ cup black beans, rinsed and drained
¼ cup chopped red bell pepper
2 tbsp chopped cilantro

For the dressing:

2 tbsp lime juice
1 tbsp olive oil
½ tsp chili powder
Salt and pepper to taste

1. In a large bowl, combine the avocado, corn, cabbage, black beans, bell pepper, and cilantro.
2. In a small jar, shake or whisk together lime juice, olive oil, chili powder, salt, and pepper.
3. Drizzle dressing over the bowl and toss gently.
4. Serve immediately, or chill for a few minutes for extra crunch.

Add grilled tofu or hemp seeds for extra protein.

Avocado Tuna Protein Salad

SERVES 4

Low-carb and high energy.

30 ⏱ | lf | gf

prep time: **15 minutes**

cook time: **None**

1 (5 oz) can tuna, drained
1 ripe avocado, diced
1 cup chopped cucumber
½ cup cherry tomatoes, halved
2 tbsp red onion, finely chopped
1 tbsp lemon juice
1 tsp olive oil
Salt and pepper to taste
Optional: chopped parsley or dill

1. In a medium bowl, mash avocado slightly.
2. Add tuna, cucumber, tomatoes, onion, lemon juice, olive oil, salt, and pepper.
3. Mix gently until combined.
4. Serve as is, in lettuce wraps, or over greens.

Great for meal prep.
Just keep the avocado separate until ready to eat.

Zucchini Noodle Thai Crunch

SERVES 2

Ideal for hot days or fast dinners that feel vibrant and clean.

nc | df | vgn

prep time: **15 minutes**

cook time: **None**

2 medium zucchinis, spiralized
½ cup shredded carrots
½ red bell pepper, julienned
¼ cup chopped cilantro
2 tbsp chopped peanuts or cashews

For the dressing:
1½ tbsp peanut butter (or almond butter)
1 tbsp lime juice
1 tsp soy sauce or tamari
1 tsp maple syrup
1-2 tbsp warm water to thin
Pinch of chili flakes or grated ginger

1. Spiralize zucchini into noodles and place in a large bowl.
2. Add carrots, bell pepper, and cilantro.
3. In a small bowl, whisk all dressing ingredients until smooth.
4. Toss veggies with dressing and top with peanuts.
5. Serve immediately or chill for a deeper flavor.

This is great for meal prep. Just keep the avocado separate until ready to eat.

Slim-Down Black Bean & Greens

SERVES 6

Balanced, bold, and metabolism-friendly.

lf | gf | vgn

prep time: **15 minutes**

cook time: **None**

2 cups cooked black beans (or 1½ cans, rinsed)
4 cups mixed greens (spinach, kale, arugula)
1 cup chopped cucumber
1 cup cherry tomatoes, halved
½ avocado, diced
¼ cup chopped red onion

For the dressing:
2 tbsp lime juice
1 tbsp olive oil
½ tsp ground cumin
Salt and pepper to taste

1. In a large bowl, combine beans, greens, cucumber, tomatoes, avocado, and onion.

2. In a separate bowl, whisk together lime juice, olive oil, cumin, salt, and pepper.

3. Pour dressing over the bowl and toss to coat evenly.

4. Serve immediately or portion into containers for meal prep.

This salad holds up beautifully for 2-3 days.
Add quinoa or grilled veggies to make it heartier.

Berry Almond Crunch Salad

SERVES 4

Packed with superfoods, perfect for leftovers.

nc | lf | vgn

prep time: **10 minutes**

cook time: **None**

4 cups mixed greens (spinach, arugula, or spring mix)
1 cup mixed berries (strawberries, blueberries, raspberries)
¼ cup sliced almonds, lightly toasted
¼ cup thinly sliced red onion (optional)
1 tbsp olive oil
1 tbsp balsamic vinegar or lemon juice
Salt and pepper to taste

1. In a large salad bowl, combine the greens, berries, onion (if using), and almonds.
2. Drizzle with olive oil and balsamic vinegar.
3. Toss gently to combine, then season with salt and pepper.
4. Serve immediately, or refrigerate without dressing for up to 1 day.

For extra protein, add hemp seeds or quinoa.

Lemony Radish Salad

SERVES 6

Great on its own or tucked into wraps.

nc | nf | vgn

prep time: **10 minutes**

cook time: **None**

2 cups thinly sliced radishes
1 tbsp lemon juice
1 tbsp olive oil
1 tsp apple cider vinegar
Salt and black pepper to taste
Optional: chopped parsley or mint for garnish

1. In a bowl, toss sliced radishes with lemon juice, vinegar, olive oil, salt, and pepper.
2. Let sit for 5-10 minutes to allow the flavor to develop and soften the radishes slightly.
3. Sprinkle with fresh herbs before serving, if desired.

For a more filling version, add cucumber, shredded carrots, or serve over a bed of arugula or baby kale.

Simple Jicama Salad

SERVES 4

Simple salad with serious bite

nc | df | vgn

prep time: **10 minutes**

cook time: **None**

1½ cups peeled and julienned jicama
½ cup chopped cucumber
1 tbsp lime juice
1 tsp olive oil
Salt and pepper to taste
Optional: pinch of chili powder or smoked paprika

1. In a medium bowl, combine jicama and cucumber.
2. Drizzle with lime juice and olive oil.
3. Add salt, pepper, and chili powder if using.
4. Toss and chill for 10 minutes before serving.

This salad stays crisp for up to 2 days. It's great for mindful eating, summer detox, or crunchy snacking on the go.

Apple Almond Crunch Salad

SERVES 3

Wholesome and simply satisfying.

nc | df | vgt

prep time: **10 minutes**

cook time: **None**

1 large apple, thinly sliced or julienned
2 cups mixed greens or spinach
¼ cup sliced almonds, lightly toasted
1 tbsp olive oil
1 tbsp lemon juice or apple cider vinegar
Salt and black pepper to taste
Optional: 1 tsp honey or maple syrup for a touch of sweetness

1. In a bowl, combine apples, greens, and almonds.
2. In a small jar, shake olive oil, lemon juice, salt, pepper, and optional sweetener.
3. Drizzle over salad and toss to coat.
4. Serve immediately to preserve crunch.

Pairs well with cooked quinoa or lentils for a more filling variation. Great for easy prep and real food snacking.

Healthy Chickpea Salad

SERVES 4

Incredibly meal-prep friendly.

30 ⏱ | gf | vgn

prep time: **15 minutes**

cook time: **None**

1½ cups cooked or canned chickpeas, rinsed
1 cup diced cucumber
½ cup cherry tomatoes, halved
¼ red onion, chopped
2 tbsp chopped parsley
1 tbsp olive oil
1 tbsp lemon juice
Salt and pepper to taste
Optional: dash of cumin or chili flakes

1. Combine chickpeas, cucumber, tomatoes, onion, and parsley in a bowl.
2. Drizzle with olive oil and lemon juice.
3. Season with salt, pepper, and optional spices.
4. Toss and chill before serving, or enjoy immediately.

Serve over greens or stuff into a pita for a portable plant-powered lunch. Keeps well for 2-3 days in the fridge.

Cauliflower Mock Potato Salad

SERVES 4

Gut-friendly and picnic-ready

lf | gf | vgn

prep time:
15 minutes

cook time:
10 minutes
(to steam cauliflower)

1 medium head cauliflower, cut into small florets
¼ cup diced celery
¼ cup finely chopped red onion
2 tbsp chopped dill pickles
¼ cup vegan mayo or plain Greek yogurt
1 tsp Dijon mustard
1 tsp lemon juice
Salt and pepper to taste
Optional: sprinkle of paprika or chopped parsley for garnish

1. Steam cauliflower florets until just fork-tender (about 8-10 minutes). Drain and cool completely.
2. In a large bowl, combine cooled cauliflower with celery, onion, and pickles.
3. In a small bowl, mix mayo, mustard, lemon juice, salt, and pepper.
4. Fold dressing into the salad and stir gently.
5. Chill before serving. Garnish as desired.

Add chopped hard-boiled eggs or avocado for a boost, or keep it light and vegan as-is.

CHAPTER 5

FALL FIBER & IMMUNE BOOST SALADS

Avocado Kale Quinoa Salad

SERVES 4

A powerhouse of superfoods for a nutrient-dense meal.

gf | df | vgn

prep time: **15 minutes**

cook time: **15 minutes** (to cook quinoa)

1 bunch kale, stems removed, leaves chopped
1 avocado, diced
1½ cups cooked quinoa
½ cup cherry tomatoes, halved
2 tbsp lemon juice
1 tbsp olive oil
Salt and pepper to taste
Optional: 1 tbsp hemp seeds or sunflower seeds

1. In a large bowl, massage kale with olive oil and lemon juice until softened.
2. Add quinoa, avocado, and cherry tomatoes.
3. Toss to combine and season with salt and pepper.
4. Sprinkle with seeds and serve fresh or chilled.

This salad stores well for 2 days. Great as a stand-alone lunch or served alongside roasted veggies or grilled tofu.

Kale Caesar Salad

SERVES 4

All the richness of the classic meal with the benefits of greens.

h | df | vgt

prep time:
10 minutes

cook time:
None

4 cups chopped kale (stems removed)
¼ cup grated Parmesan or nutritional yeast
1 cup croutons (whole grain or gluten-free)

For the dressing:
¼ cup plain Greek yogurt (or plant-based yogurt)
1 tbsp lemon juice
1 tsp Dijon mustard
1 tsp olive oil.
1 garlic clove, finely minced
Salt and pepper to taste

1. Massage kale with a touch of olive oil until softened (1-2 minutes).
2. In a small bowl, whisk together all dressing ingredients until smooth.
3. Toss kale with dressing, then top with croutons and Parmesan (or nutritional yeast).
4. Serve immediately or let sit for 10 minutes to mellow the flavor.

Loaded wih antioxidants. Add roasted chickpeas for crunch or grilled protein for a full meal.

Spinach Blackberry Salad

SERVES 4

Effortlessly beautiful and perfect for lunch or entertaining.

30 | h | lf | nf | sf

prep time: **10 minutes**

cook time: **None**

6 cups baby spinach leaves
1½ cups fresh blackberries
½ small red onion, thinly sliced
¼ cup sunflower seeds or pumpkin seeds
¼ cup crumbled feta (or omit for dairy-free)
2 tbsp balsamic vinegar
1 tbsp olive oil
1 tsp honey or maple syrup
Salt and black pepper to taste

1. Place the spinach, blackberries, and red onion in a large bowl.
2. In a separate bowl or jar, whisk together the balsamic vinegar, olive oil, honey or maple syrup, salt, and pepper.
3. Drizzle the dressing over the salad and toss gently to combine.
4. Top with seeds and feta just before serving.

Add grilled chicken or quinoa to turn this into a main dish.

Avocado Spinach Mint Salad

SERVES 4

A simple way to cool down and nourish up on warm days.

h | nc | nf | sf

prep time: **12 minutes**

cook time: **None**

4 cups fresh spinach
1 ripe avocado, cubed
¼ cup fresh mint leaves, torn
2 tbsp lemon juice
1 tbsp olive oil
½ tsp honey
Pinch of salt
Optional: chopped pistachios or hemp seeds for texture

1. Toss the spinach, avocado, and mint together in a serving bowl.
2. In a small jar, shake the lemon juice, olive oil, honey, and salt until emulsified.
3. Drizzle the dressing over the salad and toss gently to combine.
4. Sprinkle with pistachios or hemp seeds just before serving, if using.

Great as a palate cleanser or paired with grilled seafood. It's cooling, healthy, and comes together in minutes.

Super Seven Spinach Salad

SERVES 5

A super salad for busy days

h | df | sf | lf

prep time: **10 minutes**

cook time: **None**

5 cups fresh spinach
1 cup cherry tomatoes, halved
½ cup sliced cucumbers
½ cup shredded carrots
¼ cup toasted almonds
1 ripe avocado, diced
2 tbsp lemon vinaigrette

1. Layer spinach, tomatoes, cucumbers, carrots, almonds, and avocado in a large bowl.

2. Drizzle with lemon vinaigrette just before serving.

3. Toss gently and serve immediately for best texture.

Feel free to swap in other raw veggies or add a sprinkle of hemp seeds. Keeps well for 1-2 hours dressed if needed.

Kale Apple Crunch Salad

SERVES 2

Bold greens, bright flavor.

gf | h | df | sf

prep time: **10 minutes**

cook time: **None**

3 cups chopped kale (stems removed)
1 apple, thinly sliced
2 tbsp chopped walnuts
1 tbsp lemon juice
1 tsp maple syrup
1 tsp olive oil
Pinch of salt

1. Massage kale with a few drops of olive oil and a pinch of salt for 1-2 minutes until softened.

2. Add apple slices and walnuts to the kale.

3. Whisk lemon juice, maple syrup, and remaining olive oil in a small bowl.

4. Drizzle dressing over the salad and toss to combine.

Add raisins or sunflower seeds for extra sweetness and crunch. Holds up well for packed lunches.

Chopped Kale with Tofu

SERVES 3

Great as a meal or energizing side.

vgt | h | df | sf

prep time: **15 minutes**

cook time: **8 minutes**

4 cups chopped kale
1 block firm tofu, pressed and cubed
1 tbsp sesame oil
2 tsp low-sodium soy sauce
1 tsp cornstarch
2 tbsp rice vinegar
1 tbsp olive oil
1 tsp grated fresh ginger
1 tsp maple syrup
Sesame seeds for topping

1. Toss tofu cubes with soy sauce and cornstarch, then pan-fry in sesame oil until crisp on all sides.

2. In a bowl, whisk together rice vinegar, olive oil, ginger, and maple syrup.

3. Massage the kale until slightly softened, then combine with tofu and dressing.

4. Top with sesame seeds and serve warm or chilled.

Tofu can be air-fried for extra crunch.
This salad holds up well for meal prep too.

Sunflower Kale Salad

SERVES 4

Earthy greens with nutty crunch.

h | df | sf | lf

prep time:
10 minutes

cook time:
None

5 cups chopped kale
¼ cup toasted sunflower seeds
¼ cup grated carrot
2 tbsp lemon juice
1 tbsp olive oil
½ tsp Dijon mustard
Salt and pepper to taste

1. Massage kale with a touch of olive oil until tender.
2. In a small bowl, whisk together lemon juice, mustard, remaining olive oil, salt, and pepper.
3. Toss kale with grated carrot and sunflower seeds.
4. Drizzle with dressing and mix well before serving.

Make it a meal with chickpeas or grilled halloumi.
This one's perfect for light lunches or picnic spreads.

Spinach Orzo Salad

SERVES 4

Pasta and greens, perfectly paired.

vgt | h | sf

prep time: **10 minutes**

cook time: **8 minutes**

1 cup dry orzo pasta
4 cups baby spinach
½ cup cherry tomatoes, halved
¼ cup chopped red onion
¼ cup crumbled feta
2 tbsp red wine vinegar
1 tbsp olive oil
1 tsp dried oregano
Salt and pepper to taste

1. Cook orzo according to package directions, then rinse under cool water and drain well.

2. In a large bowl, combine spinach, tomatoes, onion, and feta.

3. Whisk together red wine vinegar, olive oil, oregano, salt, and pepper.

4. Toss the orzo and vegetables with the dressing until fully coated.

5. Serve at room temperature or chill before serving.

Add olives or chickpeas for variation.
Holds well for potlucks and next-day lunches.

Strawberry Spinach Salad

SERVES 2

Perfect as a starter or light lunch.

gf | h | df | lf

prep time: **8 minutes**

cook time: **None**

3 cups baby spinach
1 cup fresh strawberries, sliced
2 tbsp sliced almonds
1 tbsp balsamic vinegar
1 tsp olive oil
½ tsp honey
Pinch of sea salt

1. Gently toss spinach and strawberries in a mixing bowl.
2. In a small dish, whisk balsamic vinegar, olive oil, honey, and salt until smooth.
3. Drizzle dressing over salad and toss lightly.
4. Sprinkle with sliced almonds just before serving.

Great with goat cheese or grilled chicken for a fuller plate. Make just before serving for best texture.

CHAPTER 6

FALL MEAL & WELLNESS BOWLS

Golden Beet & Pomegranate Salad

SERVES 3

Vibrant salad with natural sweetness.

gf | h | df | sf

prep time:
15 minutes

cook time:
40 minutes
(for the beets)

3 medium golden beets, roasted and sliced
2 cups arugula or baby spinach
½ cup pomegranate seeds
2 tbsp chopped walnuts
2 tbsp orange juice
1 tbsp olive oil
½ tsp honey
Pinch of salt and black pepper

1. Roast golden beets at 400°F for 35-40 minutes, then let cool and slice.
2. In a bowl, whisk together orange juice, olive oil, honey, salt, and pepper.
3. Toss arugula, beets, and pomegranate seeds with dressing.
4. Top with chopped walnuts before serving.

Substitute blood orange juice for extra depth or add goat cheese for creaminess. Eye-catching and nutrient-dense.

Pomegranate Feta Salad

SERVES 4

A colorful holiday favorite.

vgt | h | gf

prep time: **10 minutes**

cook time: **None**

4 cups mixed salad greens
½ cup pomegranate seeds
¼ cup crumbled feta
¼ cup thinly sliced red onion
2 tbsp balsamic vinegar
1 tbsp olive oil
Salt and pepper to taste

1. Combine salad greens, pomegranate seeds, feta, and red onion in a bowl.
2. In a separate dish, whisk together balsamic vinegar, olive oil, salt, and pepper.
3. Drizzle dressing over salad and toss gently to combine.
4. Serve immediately for best texture.

Add roasted nuts or quinoa to bulk it up.
This salad brings brightness to any meal.

Mandarin Orange Salad

SERVES 4

Easy, refreshing, and feels like a burst of sunshine on your plate.

gf | h | df | sf

prep time: **10 minutes**

cook time: **None**

4 cups mixed greens or romaine
1 cup mandarin orange segments (fresh or drained canned)
¼ cup sliced almonds
¼ cup thinly sliced red onion
2 tbsp orange juice
1 tbsp apple cider vinegar
1 tsp olive oil
½ tsp maple syrup
Salt to taste

1. In a large bowl, combine greens, mandarin segments, red onion, and almonds.
2. In a small jar, shake orange juice, vinegar, olive oil, maple syrup, and salt until combined.
3. Pour dressing over salad and toss gently to coat.
4. Serve chilled or at room temperature.

Try adding grilled chicken or edamame for a protein boost. Pairs well with Asian-inspired meals.

Fennel Mint Slaw

SERVES 2

A fresh twist on classic slaw.

gf | h | df | sf | lf

prep time: **12 minutes**

cook time: **None**

1 medium fennel bulb, thinly sliced
¼ cup mint leaves, torn
1 tbsp lemon juice
1 tbsp olive oil
¼ tsp honey
Salt and black pepper to taste

1. Toss sliced fennel and mint leaves in a bowl.
2. In a small cup, whisk lemon juice, olive oil, honey, salt, and pepper.
3. Pour dressing over the slaw and mix well.
4. Let sit for 5-10 minutes before serving to mellow the flavors.

Add shaved apple or radish for variety.
This is a crisp, light addition to any meal rotation.

Blueberry Peach Salad

SERVES 3

Summer flavors in every bite.

gf | h | vgt | sf

prep time: **10 minutes**

cook time: **None**

3 cups mixed greens
1 ripe peach, sliced thin
½ cup fresh blueberries
2 tbsp chopped pecans or walnuts
1 tbsp lime juice
1 tbsp olive oil
1 tsp honey
Pinch of sea salt

1. Place greens, peach slices, and blueberries in a salad bowl.
2. In a small jar, combine lime juice, olive oil, honey, and salt. Shake well.
3. Drizzle the dressing over the salad and toss gently.
4. Top with chopped nuts just before serving.

Naturally sweet and antioxidant-rich.
Great with grilled halloumi or as a fresh brunch addition.

Asian Apple Slaw

SERVES 4

Sweet apple, crisp slaw, tangy bite.

gf | h | df | sf

prep time: **12 minutes**

cook time: **None**

2 cups shredded green cabbage
1 cup shredded red cabbage
1 medium apple, julienned
2 tbsp chopped green onion
1 tbsp rice vinegar
1 tbsp olive oil or sesame oil
1 tsp grated ginger
½ tsp honey
Pinch of salt

1. Toss green and red cabbage with julienned apple and green onion in a large bowl.
2. In a separate cup, whisk together rice vinegar, oil, ginger, honey, and salt.
3. Pour dressing over the slaw and mix thoroughly.
4. Let sit for 10 minutes before serving to enhance flavor.

Try adding toasted sesame seeds or crushed peanuts.

Avocado Lime Black Bean Salad

SERVES 4

A Tex-Mex inspired power salad.

vgt | h | df | gf

prep time: **10 min utes**

cook time: **None**

1 can black beans, drained and rinsed
1 ripe avocado, diced
1 cup cherry tomatoes, halved
¼ cup chopped red onion
2 tbsp chopped cilantro
2 tbsp lime juice
1 tbsp olive oil
Salt and pepper to tast

1. Combine black beans, avocado, tomatoes, onion, and cilantro in a large bowl.
2. Whisk together lime juice, olive oil, salt, and pepper in a small dish.
3. Pour the dressing over the salad and toss gently to combine.
4. Serve immediately or chill for 15 minutes to deepen flavor.

Great with tortilla chips or served in lettuce cups.

Avocado Chickpea Bowl

SERVES 4

Power bowl with texture and color.

vgt | h | df | sf

prep time: **12 minutes**

cook time: **None**

1 can chickpeas, drained and rinsed
1 ripe avocado, sliced
1 cup shredded carrots
1 cup chopped cucumber
½ cup cherry tomatoes, halved
1 tbsp lemon juice
1 tbsp tahini
1 tsp olive oil
Salt and pepper to taste

1. Arrange chickpeas, avocado, carrots, cucumber, and tomatoes in a wide bowl.
2. In a small cup, whisk lemon juice, tahini, olive oil, salt, and pepper until smooth.
3. Drizzle dressing over the bowl and toss just before serving.
4. Enjoy immediately or pack for a portable lunch.

Great served cold or at room temperature.
Top with pumpkin seeds or sprouts for extra crunch.

Cold Veggie Noodle Salad

SERVES 4

Chilled noodles, crisp veggies, tangy sauce.

vgt | h | df | sf

prep time: X

cook time: None

6 oz rice noodles or soba noodles
1 cup shredded carrots
1 cup thinly sliced cucumber
½ cup shredded red cabbage
2 tbsp chopped scallions
2 tbsp rice vinegar
1 tbsp soy sauce
1 tsp sesame oil
½ tsp maple syrup
Optional: sesame seeds for garnish

1. Cook noodles according to package instructions, then rinse under cold water and drain well.

2. In a large bowl, toss noodles with carrots, cucumber, cabbage, and scallions.

3. In a small jar, combine rice vinegar, soy sauce, sesame oil, and maple syrup. Shake or whisk until blended.

4. Pour dressing over noodle mixture and toss to coat evenly.

5. Sprinkle with sesame seeds if desired, and serve chilled.

Add edamame or tofu for a protein boost. This salad travels well and keeps in the fridge for 1-2 days.

Orange Beet Salad

SERVES 3

A vibrant, winter-spring crossover.

gf | h | df | sf

prep time: X

cook time: None

2 medium beets, roasted and sliced
1 large orange, peeled and segmented
2 cups baby arugula or spinach
¼ cup chopped walnuts
1 tbsp orange juice
1 tbsp olive oil
½ tsp Dijon mustard
Salt and pepper to taste

1. Roast beets at 400°F until tender, then let cool and slice.
2. In a mixing bowl, combine sliced beets, orange segments, and greens.
3. Whisk together orange juice, olive oil, mustard, salt, and pepper to create the dressing.
4. Drizzle dressing over the salad and toss gently.
5. Top with walnuts and serve fresh.

X

CHAPTER 7

WINTER WARM SALADS

Roasted Veggie Lentil Jar Salad

SERVES 4

Layers of flavor, ready to go

vgt | h | df | sf

prep time: **15 minutes**

cook time: **30 minutes**

1 cup cooked green or brown lentils
1 small zucchini, chopped
1 bell pepper, chopped
½ red onion, sliced
1 tbsp olive oil
2 cups baby spinach
2 tbsp balsamic vinegar
1 tsp Dijon mustard
Salt and pepper to taste

1. Roast zucchini, bell pepper, and onion at 400°F with olive oil, salt, and pepper for about 25-30 minutes until tender. Let cool.

2. In a small bowl, whisk together balsamic vinegar, mustard, salt, and pepper for the dressing.

3. To assemble, layer dressing first in the jar, followed by lentils, roasted vegetables, and top with spinach.

4. Seal and refrigerate. Shake before eating or pour into a bowl and toss.

Customize with roasted sweet potato or chickpeas.

Roasted Beet & Lentil Bowl

SERVES 3

Warm and grounding grain-free bowl.

gf | h | df | sf

prep time: **15 minutes**

cook time: **40 minutes**

2 medium beets, roasted and chopped
1½ cups cooked green lentils
2 cups arugula or baby spinach
1 tbsp tahini
1 tbsp lemon juice
1 tsp olive oil
½ tsp maple syrup
Salt and black pepper to taste

1. Roast beets at 400°F until fork-tender, about 35-40 minutes, then let cool and chop.

2. In a bowl, whisk together tahini, lemon juice, olive oil, maple syrup, salt, and pepper until smooth.

3. Arrange greens in serving bowls and top with lentils and roasted beets.

4. Drizzle with dressing just before serving.

Serve warm or cold. Add toasted pumpkin seeds or goat cheese if desired. Filling and perfect for batch prep.

Mushroom Spinach Salad

SERVES 3

A bistro-style salad at home.

vgt | h | sf

prep time: **10 minutes**

cook time: **10 minutes**

4 cups baby spinach
1½ cups sliced mushrooms (cremini or button)
1 tbsp olive oil
1 tsp balsamic vinegar
¼ cup grated parmesan or nutritional yeast
Salt and black pepper to taste

1. Heat olive oil in a skillet over medium heat, then sauté mushrooms until golden and tender, about 7-8 minutes.
2. Add balsamic vinegar, stir, and remove from heat.
3. Place spinach in a bowl and top with warm mushrooms.
4. Sprinkle with parmesan or nutritional yeast and season with salt and pepper.

Best served immediately while mushrooms are warm. Add a soft-boiled egg or pine nuts for extra depth.

Broccoli Slaw with Cranberry Orange

SERVES 4

Great for potlucks or prep.

gf | h | df | sf

prep time: **12 minutes**

cook time: **None**

3 cups shredded broccoli stems or pre-cut slaw mix
⅓ cup dried cranberries
1 small carrot, shredded
1 tbsp orange juice
1 tbsp apple cider vinegar
1 tsp olive oil
½ tsp maple syrup
Salt and pepper to taste

1. Combine broccoli slaw, cranberries, and shredded carrot in a large bowl.
2. Whisk together orange juice, vinegar, olive oil, maple syrup, salt, and pepper.
3. Pour dressing over slaw and toss well.
4. Let sit for 10 minutes before serving to absorb flavor.

Add chopped almonds or sunflower seeds for texture. This salad keeps well in the fridge for up to two days.

Bulgur & Quinoa Salad

SERVES 4

Hearty grains, fresh herbs, zesty bite.

vgt | h | df | sf
SERVES 4

prep time: **15 minutes**

cook time: **20 minutes**

½ cup bulgur, cooked and cooled
½ cup quinoa, cooked and cooled
1 cup cherry tomatoes, halved
½ cucumber, diced
¼ cup chopped parsley
2 tbsp lemon juice
1 tbsp olive oil
Salt and pepper to taste

1. Combine bulgur, quinoa, tomatoes, cucumber, and parsley in a mixing bowl.
2. In a small jar, shake together lemon juice, olive oil, salt, and pepper.
3. Pour dressing over the salad and toss gently to combine.
4. Serve chilled or at room temperature.

Add chickpeas or feta to boost protein. This dish holds up beautifully for a few days in the fridge.

Gado Gado

SERVES 3

Indonesian bowl of bold textures.

gf | h | vgt

prep time: **20 minutes**

cook time: **10 minutes**

1 cup green beans, steamed
1 cup shredded cabbage
1 small potato, boiled and sliced
½ cup cucumber slices
1 hard-boiled egg, halved
½ block tofu, pan-seared
2 tbsp peanut butter
1 tbsp soy sauce
1 tbsp lime juice
1 tsp maple syrup
Hot water to thin sauce
Chili flakes (optional)

1. Arrange green beans, cabbage, potato, cucumber, egg, and tofu on a large plate or shallow bowl.

2. In a small bowl, whisk peanut butter, soy sauce, lime juice, maple syrup, and enough hot water to make a pourable sauce.

3. Drizzle sauce generously over the ingredients.

4. Sprinkle with chili flakes if desired and serve immediately.

Gado Gado is endlessly flexible.
Customize with tempeh, sprouts, or carrots.

Tomato Mozzarella Salad

SERVES 2

Elegant, easy, and always fresh.

gf | h | vgt | sf

prep time: **8 minutes**

cook time: **None**

2 large ripe tomatoes, sliced
4 oz fresh mozzarella, sliced
¼ cup fresh basil leaves
1 tbsp olive oil
1 tsp balsamic glaze or vinegar
Salt and black pepper to taste

1. Arrange tomato and mozzarella slices on a plate, alternating in layers.
2. Tuck fresh basil leaves between slices.
3. Drizzle with olive oil and balsamic glaze.
4. Sprinkle with salt and freshly cracked black pepper before serving.

Use heirloom tomatoes for extra color and flavor.
Serve with crusty bread or on a bed of greens.

Avocado Arugula Salad

SERVES 4

A fresh, minimalist dish that complements nearly anything.

h | df | gf | sf

prep time: **7 minutes**

cook time: **None**

3 cups arugula
1 ripe avocado, sliced
1 tbsp lemon juice
1 tbsp olive oil
Salt and black pepper to taste

1. Place arugula and avocado in a mixing bowl.
2. In a small dish, whisk lemon juice, olive oil, salt, and pepper.
3. Drizzle dressing over salad and toss gently.
4. Serve immediately for peak freshness.

Add shaved parmesan or roasted seeds for extra texture. This pairs beautifully with pasta or grilled dishes.

Roasted Cauliflower Chickpea Bowl

SERVES 4

Warm spices and bold flavor in a fiber-packed bowl.

vgt | h | df | gf

prep time: **10 minutes**

cook time: **30 minutes**

1 small head cauliflower, cut into florets
1 can chickpeas, drained and rinsed
1 tbsp olive oil
1 tsp cumin
1 tsp paprika
½ tsp garlic powder
2 cups baby spinach or cooked quinoa
Salt and pepper to taste
Optional: tahini drizzle or lemon wedges

1. Toss cauliflower and chickpeas with olive oil and spices on a baking sheet.
2. Roast at 400°F for 25-30 minutes, shaking halfway, until golden and crisp.
3. Arrange greens or quinoa in serving bowls.
4. Top with the roasted mixture and a drizzle of tahini or fresh lemon.

Meal prep-friendly and endlessly customizable. Try it with avocado or pickled onions for extra flavor layers.

Sweet Potato Lentil Bowl

SERVES 3

Hearty, earthy, and naturally sweet for cooler days.

gf | h | df | sf

prep time: **15 minutes**

cook time: **30 minutes**

1 medium sweet potato, peeled and cubed
1 tbsp olive oil
1 cup cooked green or brown lentils
2 cups spinach or cooked rice
1 tbsp tahini
1 tbsp lemon juice
1 tsp maple syrup
Salt and pepper to taste

1. Toss sweet potato cubes with olive oil, salt, and pepper. Roast at 400°F for 25-30 minutes.
2. In a small bowl, whisk together tahini, lemon juice, maple syrup, salt, and pepper.
3. Assemble bowls with spinach or rice, lentils, and roasted sweet potato.
4. Drizzle with the dressing and serve warm or at room temp.

Add toasted pumpkin seeds or avocado for richness.
Stores well and reheats beautifully.

CHAPTER 8

YEAR-ROUND VEGAN, GLUTEN-FREE & DAIRY-FREE

Edamame Cabbage Crunch Salad

SERVES 4

Protein-packed, super crunchy salad.

vgt | h | df | gf

prep time: **12 minutes**

cook time: **5 minutes** (edamame)

2 cups shredded green cabbage
1 cup cooked and shelled edamame
½ cup shredded carrot
2 tbsp chopped cilantro
1 tbsp lime juice
1 tbsp sesame oil
1 tsp rice vinegar
Salt and pepper to taste
Optional: sesame seeds for topping

1. In a large bowl, toss together cabbage, edamame, carrots, and cilantro.
2. Whisk lime juice, sesame oil, rice vinegar, salt, and pepper in a small cup.
3. Pour dressing over the salad and mix well.
4. Top with sesame seeds if desired and serve chilled.

Great for packed lunches or picnics. Add soba noodles or crushed peanuts for variation.

Spicy Cucumber Chickpea Salad

SERVES 2

A no-cook salad with kick.

vgt | h | df | sf

prep time: **8 minutes**

cook time: **None**

1 can chickpeas, drained and rinsed
1 cup chopped cucumber
2 tbsp chopped red onion
1 tbsp lime juice
1 tsp olive oil
½ tsp chili flakes or hot sauce
Salt to taste
Optional: chopped cilantro for garnish

1. Combine chickpeas, cucumber, and onion in a bowl.
2. In a small dish, whisk together lime juice, olive oil, chili, and salt.
3. Pour dressing over salad and mix to coat evenly.
4. Garnish with cilantro and serve immediately or chill briefly.

Adjust spice to your liking.
This salad pairs well with wraps or grain bowls.

Zucchini Salad with Lemon

SERVES 2

Light, tangy, and surprisingly satisfying—perfect as a crisp side.

X

prep time: **10 minutes**

cook time: **None**

2 medium zucchini, shaved into ribbons
1 tbsp lemon juice
1 tsp olive oil
1 tsp chopped fresh parsley
Salt and pepper to taste
Optional: shaved parmesan or pine nuts

1. Use a vegetable peeler to create thin zucchini ribbons and place them in a bowl.
2. Whisk lemon juice, olive oil, parsley, salt, and pepper in a small dish.
3. Drizzle over zucchini and toss gently to coat.
4. Add parmesan or pine nuts just before serving if desired.

Let sit for 5-10 minutes before serving to soften slightly. A simple and elegant summer dish.

Spinach Salad

SERVES 3

Endlessly adaptable.

vgt | h | gf | sf

prep time: **5 minutes**

cook time: x

4 cups baby spinach
1 tbsp lemon juice
1 tbsp olive oil
½ tsp honey or maple syrup
Salt and black pepper to taste

1. Place baby spinach in a large salad bowl.
2. In a small cup, whisk lemon juice, olive oil, sweetener, salt, and pepper.
3. Drizzle dressing over spinach and toss to coat.
4. Serve as-is or build on it with nuts, cheese, or fruit.

Great with sliced strawberries, crumbled feta, or toasted almonds. A flexible favorite.

Greek Salad with Rice

SERVES 4

Mediterranean flavor with a hearty grain

vgt | h | sf

prep time: **15 minutes**

cook time: **15 minutes** (rice)

1 cup cooked and cooled white or brown rice
1 cup cherry tomatoes, halved
1 cup chopped cucumber
¼ cup diced red onion
¼ cup crumbled feta
2 tbsp chopped olives
1 tbsp red wine vinegar
1 tbsp olive oil
1 tsp dried oregano
Salt and pepper to taste

1. Combine rice, tomatoes, cucumber, red onion, feta, and olives in a large bowl.

2. In a small dish, whisk together vinegar, olive oil, oregano, salt, and pepper.

3. Pour dressing over salad and toss to combine.

4. Chill before serving or enjoy at room temperature.

Add chickpeas for extra protein.
Travels well and keeps for 2-3 days in the fridge.

Healthy Tuna Salad

SERVES 2

High in protein and easy to whip up.

gf | h | df | sf

prep time: **10 minutes**

cook time: **None**

1 can tuna, drained
½ cup chopped cucumber
¼ cup chopped celery
2 tbsp chopped red onion
1 tbsp lemon juice
1 tbsp olive oil
Salt and pepper to taste
Optional: chopped parsley or capers

1. Place tuna in a mixing bowl and break it up with a fork.
2. Add cucumber, celery, and red onion, and mix gently.
3. Drizzle with lemon juice and olive oil, then season with salt and pepper.
4. Stir until evenly combined. Add herbs or capers if desired.

Serve in lettuce wraps, on whole grain toast, or with crackers.

Avocado Heirloom Tomato Salad

SERVES 2

Simple, refreshing, and perfect for warm-weather meals.

gf | h | df | sf

prep time: **7 minutes**

cook time: **None**

2 large heirloom tomatoes, sliced
1 ripe avocado, sliced
¼ tsp sea salt
1 tbsp olive oil
Freshly ground black pepper to taste
Optional: fresh basil or microgreens

1. Arrange tomato and avocado slices on a plate, slightly overlapping.
2. Sprinkle with salt and freshly cracked pepper.
3. Drizzle with olive oil and garnish with basil or microgreens if using.
4. Serve immediately for best texture and flavor.

Pairs well with grilled bread or chilled white wine.

Simple Macaroni Salad

SERVES 4

Packed with crunch and gentle tang, it's a perfect make-ahead for lunches, barbecues, or gatherings.

vgt | h | sf

prep time: **10 minutes**

cook time: **10 minutes**

2 cups cooked elbow macaroni, cooled
½ cup chopped bell pepper
¼ cup chopped celery
2 tbsp chopped red onion
¼ cup plain Greek yogurt or olive oil
1 tsp apple cider vinegar
½ tsp Dijon mustard
Salt and pepper to taste

1. Combine cooked macaroni, bell pepper, celery, and red onion in a large bowl.
2. In a small bowl, whisk together yogurt or olive oil, vinegar, mustard, salt, and pepper.
3. Add dressing to the salad and stir to coat evenly.
4. Chill for 30 minutes before serving, if desired.

Add peas or pickles for a flavor twist.
This salad improves as it sits.

Avocado Heirloom Tomato Salad

SERVES 2

Quick, colorful, and nutrient-rich.

gf | h | df | sf

prep time: **8 minutes**

cook time: **None**

1 large heirloom tomato, chopped
1 ripe avocado, diced
1 tbsp chopped red onion
1 tbsp olive oil
1 tsp red wine vinegar
Salt and pepper to taste
Optional: chopped fresh basil

1. Gently combine tomato, avocado, and red onion in a bowl.
2. Drizzle with olive oil and red wine vinegar.
3. Season with salt and pepper, then toss lightly to coat.
4. Garnish with fresh basil if using and serve immediately.

Adjust spice to your liking.
This salad pairs well with wraps or grain bowls.

Tofu Salad over Baby Spinach

SERVES 3

Plant-based protein with flavor.

vgt | h | df | gf

prep time: **15 minutes**

cook time: **10 minutes**

½ block firm tofu, pressed and cubed
1 tbsp soy sauce or tamari
1 tsp olive oil
4 cups baby spinach
1 tsp sesame oil
1 tbsp rice vinegar
½ tsp maple syrup
Salt and pepper to taste
Optional: sesame seeds for topping

1. Pan-sear tofu cubes in olive oil over medium heat until golden, about 8-10 minutes.
2. Drizzle tofu with soy sauce and cook 1 more minute to absorb flavor.
3. In a bowl, whisk sesame oil, rice vinegar, maple syrup, salt, and pepper.
4. Toss spinach with dressing, top with tofu, and garnish with sesame seeds if desired.

Add shredded carrot or avocado to round it out.
Tofu can also be air-fried for extra crunch.

CHAPTER 9

MINDFUL EATING & WELLNESS MEALS

Lentil Avocado Detox Bowl

SERVES 2

Clean fuel in every forkful.

gf | h | df | sf

prep time: **10 minutes**

cook time: **20 minutes** (lentils)

1 cup cooked green lentils
1 ripe avocado, sliced
1 cup baby spinach or mixed greens
½ cup shredded carrots
1 tbsp lemon juice
½ tsp turmeric
1 tbsp olive oil
Salt and black pepper to taste

1. Place greens in a shallow bowl and top with lentils, avocado slices, and shredded carrot.

2. In a small dish, whisk lemon juice, turmeric, olive oil, salt, and pepper.

3. Drizzle dressing over the bowl and toss gently.

4. Serve fresh or slightly chilled for a calming meal.

Top with hemp seeds or pumpkin seeds for extra protein and crunch.

×

Caesar Salad with Greek Yogurt

SERVES 2

Guilt-free Caesar made modern

h | sf

prep time: **10 minutes**

cook time: **None**

4 cups chopped romaine lettuce
¼ cup grated parmesan cheese
1 cup whole grain croutons
¼ cup plain Greek yogurt
1 tbsp lemon juice
1 tsp Dijon mustard
1 tsp olive oil
1 garlic clove, minced
Salt and black pepper to taste

1. Place chopped romaine in a large bowl and top with croutons and parmesan.

2. In a small bowl, whisk together Greek yogurt, lemon juice, Dijon mustard, olive oil, garlic, salt, and pepper.

3. Drizzle dressing over salad and toss well to coat.

4. Serve immediately with extra parmesan if desired.

Add grilled chicken or chickpeas for a full meal.
This Caesar is creamy, tangy, and refreshingly light.

Carrot Beet Salad

SERVES 2

Refreshing and packed with antioxidants.

gf | h | df | sf

prep time: **12 minutes**

cook time: **None**

1 medium raw beet, peeled and shredded
1 large carrot, peeled and shredded
1 tbsp orange juice
1 tsp lemon juice
1 tsp olive oil
Salt and black pepper to taste
Optional: chopped parsley or pumpkin seeds

1. Combine shredded beet and carrot in a mixing bowl.
2. In a small cup, whisk orange juice, lemon juice, olive oil, salt, and pepper.
3. Pour dressing over the salad and toss to combine.
4. Top with parsley or seeds if desired and serve fresh.

Let sit for 10 minutes to mellow the raw flavor. Works great as a crunchy sandwich filling, too.

Waldorf Chicken Salad

SERVES 4

Creamy without being heavy and loaded with natural sweetness.

gf | h

prep time: **15 minutes**

cook time: **10 minutes** (chicken)

2 cups cooked chicken breast, chopped
1 apple, diced
½ cup chopped celery
¼ cup halved red grapes or raisins
¼ cup plain Greek yogurt
1 tsp lemon juice
Salt and black pepper to taste
Optional: chopped walnuts

1. In a large bowl, combine chicken, apple, celery, and grapes.
2. In a separate dish, mix yogurt, lemon juice, salt, and pepper until smooth.
3. Add dressing to the salad and toss until evenly coated.
4. Stir in walnuts if using and serve chilled or room temp.

Serve over lettuce, in wraps, or stuffed into pita. Excellent for lunch prep or picnics.

Cold Pea Mint Salad

SERVES 3

A refreshing bite with herbal twist.

gf | h | vgt | sf

prep time: **10 minutes**

cook time: **3 minutes** (peas)

1½ cups green peas, fresh or frozen
2 tbsp chopped fresh mint
1 tbsp lemon juice
1 tsp olive oil
Salt and black pepper to taste
Optional: crumbled feta or parmesan

1. Blanch peas in boiling water for 2-3 minutes, then rinse under cold water and drain.
2. Toss peas with chopped mint in a bowl.
3. Whisk together lemon juice, olive oil, salt, and pepper.
4. Drizzle over peas and mix gently.
5. Add cheese if desired and serve chilled or at room temperature.

Perfect as a light side for grilled dishes or spring menus.

Tropical Pineapple Vinaigrette Salad

SERVES 4

A salad that tastes like an island vacation.

gf | h | df | sf

prep time: **10 minutes**

cook time: **None**

4 cups mixed greens
1 cup fresh pineapple chunks
¼ cup thinly sliced red onion
2 tbsp pineapple juice
1 tbsp apple cider vinegar
1 tbsp olive oil
½ tsp honey
Salt and pepper to taste

1. Place greens, pineapple chunks, and red onion in a large bowl.
2. In a jar, shake pineapple juice, vinegar, olive oil, honey, salt, and pepper until well combined.
3. Drizzle dressing over the salad and toss to coat.
4. Serve immediately or chill slightly before serving.

Top with grilled shrimp, coconut flakes, or avocado for a full tropical plate.

Eggplant Tomato Salad

SERVES 3

Mediterranean flavor with depth.

gf | h | df | sf

prep time: **15 minutes**
cook time: **25 minutes**

1 medium eggplant, cubed
1 cup cherry tomatoes, halved
1 tbsp olive oil
1 tsp red wine vinegar
½ tsp dried oregano
Salt and black pepper to taste
Optional: chopped parsley or fresh basil

1. Toss eggplant cubes with olive oil, salt, and pepper. Roast at 400°F for 20-25 minutes until golden and tender.

2. Let cool slightly, then combine with cherry tomatoes in a bowl.

3. Add vinegar and oregano, then toss gently to combine.

4. Garnish with herbs if desired and serve warm or chilled.

Let sit for richer flavor.
Pairs beautifully with hummus, grilled bread, or couscous.

Strawberry Romaine Salad

SERVES 4

Just right for warm-weather meals or festive gatherings.

gf | h | df | sf

prep time: **10 minutes**

cook time: **None**

4 cups chopped romaine
1 cup sliced strawberries
¼ cup thinly sliced red onion
2 tbsp apple cider vinegar
1 tbsp olive oil
1 tsp honey or maple syrup
Salt and pepper to taste

1. Combine romaine, strawberries, and red onion in a large salad bowl.
2. In a small jar, whisk together vinegar, olive oil, honey, salt, and pepper.
3. Pour dressing over the salad and toss gently to coat.
4. Serve immediately for best freshness and crunch.

Top with toasted pecans or goat cheese for extra depth.

Beet Blue Cheese Salad

SERVES 2

Bold flavors in perfect balance

gf | h | sf

prep time: **15 minutes**

cook time: **35 minutes**

2 medium beets, roasted and sliced
2 cups arugula or mixed greens
¼ cup crumbled blue cheese
2 tbsp chopped walnuts
1 tbsp balsamic vinegar
1 tbsp olive oil
Salt and black pepper to taste

1. Roast beets at 400°F for 35 minutes, then let cool and slice.
2. In a bowl, arrange greens and top with beet slices.
3. Add crumbled blue cheese and chopped walnuts.
4. Drizzle with balsamic and olive oil, then season with salt and pepper.
5. Serve chilled or at room temperature.

Add grilled chicken for a full meal.

Tomato Cucumber Salad

SERVES 2

Quick to make, cooling, and perfect for barbecues, picnics, or everyday meals.

X

prep time: **8 minutes**

cook time: **None**

2 cups chopped tomatoes
1 cup chopped cucumber
¼ cup thinly sliced red onion
1 tbsp red wine vinegar
1 tbsp olive oil
Salt and pepper to taste
Optional: chopped dill or parsley

1. Combine tomatoes, cucumber, and red onion in a serving bowl.
2. Whisk together red wine vinegar, olive oil, salt, and pepper.
3. Pour dressing over vegetables and toss gently.
4. Add herbs if using and serve immediately or after a short chill.

Adjust spice to your liking.
This salad pairs well with wraps or grain bowls.

CHAPTER 10

REAL FOOD & SIMPLE COOKING

Avocado Arugula Salad

SERVES 3

Simple, flavorful, and works perfectly as a starter or light meal.

h | df | gf | sf

prep time: **7 minutes**

cook time: **None**

3 cups arugula
1 ripe avocado, sliced
1 tbsp lemon juice
1 tbsp olive oil
Salt and black pepper to taste

1. Place arugula and avocado in a salad bowl.
2. In a small dish, whisk lemon juice, olive oil, salt, and pepper.
3. Drizzle dressing over salad and toss gently.
4. Serve immediately for best texture and freshness.

Great with grilled dishes or pasta.
Add shaved parmesan or roasted seeds for variety.

Greek Salad with Rice

SERVES 4

Full of crisp veggies, briny feta, and herbs.

vgt | h | sf

prep time: **15 minutes**

cook time: **15 minutes**

1 cup cooked and cooled brown or white rice
1 cup chopped cucumber
1 cup cherry tomatoes, halved
¼ cup diced red onion
¼ cup crumbled feta
2 tbsp chopped olives
1 tbsp lemon juice
1 tbsp olive oil
1 tsp dried oregano
Salt and pepper to taste

1. Combine rice, cucumber, tomatoes, onion, feta, and olives in a large bowl.
2. Whisk lemon juice, olive oil, oregano, salt, and pepper in a separate dish.
3. Pour dressing over salad and toss well.
4. Chill before serving or enjoy at room temperature.

Add chickpeas or parsley for variation.
Holds up great for packed lunches.

Green Bean & Cherry Tomato

SERVES 3

A bright veggie side with crunch

gf | h | df | sf

prep time: **10 minutes**

cook time: **3 minutes** (green beans)

2 cups trimmed green beans
1 cup halved cherry tomatoes
1 tbsp red wine vinegar
1 tbsp olive oil
Salt and black pepper to taste
Optional: chopped fresh basil

1. Blanch green beans in boiling water for 2-3 minutes, then transfer to ice water and drain.
2. Combine green beans and cherry tomatoes in a mixing bowl.
3. Whisk together red wine vinegar, olive oil, salt, and pepper.
4. Pour dressing over the salad and toss gently.
5. Garnish with basil if desired and serve chilled or at room temperature.

Try adding feta or white beans for extra texture.

Tomato Basil Mozzarella Salad

SERVES 2

Classic Caprese simplicity, simply served.

vgt | h | gf | sf

prep time: **8 minutes**

cook time: **None**

2 large tomatoes, sliced
4 oz fresh mozzarella, sliced
¼ cup fresh basil leaves
1 tbsp olive oil
1 tsp balsamic glaze or vinegar
Salt and black pepper to taste

1. Layer tomato and mozzarella slices on a plate, alternating.
2. Tuck basil leaves between slices.
3. Drizzle with olive oil and balsamic.
4. Season with salt and black pepper before serving.

Best served fresh. Great with crusty bread or as a side to pasta or grilled dishes.

Broccoli Cranberry Salad

SERVES 4

Crunchy, tangy, and slightly sweet potluck classic

gf | h | df | sf

prep time: **10 minutes**

cook time: **None**

3 cups chopped raw broccoli
¼ cup dried cranberries
2 tbsp sunflower seeds
2 tbsp chopped red onion
2 tbsp apple cider vinegar
1 tbsp olive oil
½ tsp maple syrup
Salt and pepper to taste

1. Combine broccoli, cranberries, sunflower seeds, and red onion in a bowl.
2. In a small dish, whisk together vinegar, olive oil, maple syrup, salt, and pepper.
3. Pour dressing over the salad and toss to coat evenly.
4. Chill for 10-15 minutes before serving.

Add shredded carrot or chopped apple for variety.
Keeps well in the fridge for 2 days.

Tomato Asparagus Salad

SERVES 3

Fresh, lemony, and perfectly light.

gf | h | df | sf

prep time: **12 minutes**

cook time: **4 minutes** (asparagus)

1 bunch asparagus, trimmed and cut into 2-inch pieces
1 cup cherry tomatoes, halved
1 tbsp lemon juice
1 tbsp olive oil
Salt and black pepper to taste
Optional: shaved parmesan or fresh herbs

1. Blanch asparagus in boiling water for 2-3 minutes, then transfer to an ice bath and drain.
2. Combine asparagus and tomatoes in a mixing bowl.
3. Whisk together lemon juice, olive oil, salt, and pepper.
4. Pour dressing over salad and toss gently.
5. Add parmesan or herbs if desired.

Add white beans for a heartier twist.
Best served chilled or at room temperature.

Spinach Mango Salad

SERVES 2

Colorful, clean, and energizing.

gf | h | df | sf

prep time: **8 minutes**

cook time: **None**

3 cups baby spinach
1 ripe mango, diced
2 tbsp chopped red onion
1 tbsp lime juice
1 tsp olive oil
Pinch of salt
Optional: fresh mint or chili flakes

1. Toss spinach, mango, and red onion in a salad bowl.
2. In a small dish, whisk lime juice, olive oil, and salt.
3. Drizzle dressing over salad and toss gently.
4. Top with mint or chili flakes if desired and serve fresh.

Add grilled shrimp or avocado for a complete meal.

Strawberry Feta Arugula Salad

SERVES 3

Beautiful, balanced, and perfect for brunches or simple lunches.

x

prep time:
10 minutes

cook time:
None

3 cups arugula
1 cup sliced strawberries
¼ cup crumbled feta
1 tbsp balsamic vinegar
1 tbsp olive oil
Salt and black pepper to taste

1. Combine arugula, strawberries, and feta in a bowl.
2. Whisk balsamic vinegar, olive oil, salt, and pepper in a small dish.
3. Drizzle dressing over the salad and toss gently to combine.
4. Serve immediately for peak freshness.

Try adding toasted almonds or cooked farro.
A perfect sweet-savory combo.

Cucumber Grape Salad

SERVES 4

Sweet-savory salad with sparkle

prep time: **10 minutes**

cook time: **None**

2 cups sliced cucumber
1 cup halved red or green grapes
2 tbsp chopped red onion
1 tbsp apple cider vinegar
1 tsp olive oil
Salt and black pepper to taste
Optional: fresh dill or mint

1. In a mixing bowl, combine cucumber, grapes, and red onion.
2. Whisk vinegar, olive oil, salt, and pepper in a small dish.
3. Pour dressing over the salad and toss gently.
4. Add herbs if using and chill before serving.

Great for picnics or potlucks.
Try with goat cheese for added richness.

Roasted Carrot & Lentil Salad

SERVES 4

A warm, comforting dish that's equally great hot or room temp.

vgt | h gf | h |

prep time: **10 minutes**

cook time: **30 minutes**

3 medium carrots, peeled and cut into sticks
1 tbsp olive oil
1 cup cooked green or brown lentils
2 cups baby spinach or arugula
1 tbsp lemon juice
1 tsp maple syrup
½ tsp ground cumin
Salt and pepper to taste

1. Toss carrot sticks in olive oil, salt, and pepper. Roast at 400°F for 25-30 minutes, until tender and caramelized.

2. In a small bowl, whisk lemon juice, maple syrup, cumin, and a pinch of salt.

3. Arrange spinach in a bowl, then layer lentils and roasted carrots on top.

4. Drizzle with the dressing and toss gently before serving.

Top with toasted seeds or some yogurt for added richness.

Get Your Free E-book!

Scan the QR code below to instantly access the e-book **'The Alkaline Juicing Starter Guide'**, absolutely free

SCAN ME

https://bonus.grapevinebooks.com/alkalinejuicing